The Prince-Bishops of Durham

by

Simon Webb

Durham, 2011

First published by The Langley Press, 2011

ISBN: 978-0-9564551-7-8

Cover picture by Miranda Brown shows Bishop Cosin's arms
above the door to his library. All other pictures reproduced by
kind permission of Durham County Council

CONTENTS

Murdered at Gateshead:
Bishop William Walcher (1071-1080)   5

Let's Build a Cathedral:
William of St Carileph (1081-1096)   11

A Bishop in the Tower:
Ranulf Flambard (1099-1128)   16

Killed by Pancake Day:
Hugh du Puiset (1153-1195)   24

A War of Attrition:
Anthony Bek (1283-1311)   28

The Golden Old Man:
Cuthbert Tunstall (1530-1559)   32

Picking Up the Pieces:
John Cosin (1660-1672)   36

Burned in Effigy:
William Van Mildert (1826-1836)   40

Durham Castle in the 18th Century

4

Murdered at Gateshead: Bishop William Walcher (1071-1080)

Of the many horsemen shown in the Bayeux Tapestry, one in particular stands out. Mounted on an eye-catching blue charger, the man has no shield, and is armed not with a spear or sword, but with a wooden club. Unlike the Norman knights, he doesn't wear a hauberk or mail coat as his top garment, but rather an item of clothing that seems to be made up of many red and black triangles. He wears the familiar conical helmet of the Norman invaders, with its 'nasal', a strip of metal to protect the nose. Under the helmet, he wears a protective hood of mail.

A glance at the Latin capitals embroidered above this anomalous figure shows him to be 'ODO EPS', Bishop Odo, holding a club and 'CONFORTAT PVEROS'; encouraging the boys. To judge from the next few metres of the Tapestry, either the 'boys' or junior soldiers didn't need encouraging, or the bishop's encouragement really worked. The Norman archers have scored so many hits on King Harold's English troops that some of them look like porcupines. Soon Harold is seen dying, with an arrow in his eye. At the end of the tapestry we see the remnant of the English running away.

If it is true that Bishop Odo commissioned the Bayeux Tapestry, and that it was made in England and shipped across the Channel to decorate his cathedral at Bayeux, then it is hardly surprising that he himself should feature on it. In fact he appears earlier, again clearly labelled, at a dinner with the future William the Conqueror. He is then seen in what may have been a select council of war before the Battle of Hastings, with William and his half-brother, Robert of Mortain.

Bishop Odo was another half-brother of William, duke of Normandy, and had been chosen as bishop of Bayeux by that future king of England. Odo played an active role in the Conquest, advising his half-brother and, thanks to his considerable wealth, supplying one hundred ships for the invasion fleet. In the Bayeux Tapestry, Odo is not shown actually fighting, and the club he holds may have been used like a commander's baton. It could also have been used as a defensive weapon: it is thought that it would have been acceptable for a bishop to use such a weapon, which would not have drawn blood as readily as would a sword, spear or axe.

After the Conquest, Odo was made earl of Kent, and may have been second only to the Conqueror in terms of power – he certainly stood in as William's deputy when his half-brother had to return to Normandy.

Odo's wealth, his political role, his willingness to go to battle and his aristocratic birth are an indication that Norman churchmen, in England or Normandy, were not as humble as some of the earlier bishops of the English, such as St Cuthbert of Lindisfarne. Odo's combination of worldly power in Kent and episcopal power in Bayeux were something his half-brother was to try to replicate near the vulnerable northern margin of England, but with the worldly and episcopal territories overlapping.

The bishop William installed at Durham was the first in a line of powerful men who would be expected to protect England by raising armies to fight against the Scots; and to negotiate with the Scots when appropriate. The bishops of Durham were also permitted to raise their own taxes, to levy tolls and customs charges, and to mint their own coins. They enjoyed complete control of the legal system in their bishopric, which was for many centuries quite separate from the legal system in the rest of England. The bishops also owned all forests, chases and warrens in the bishopric, and were considered to be senior to all other aristocrats in the area.

Although they would not have thought of themselves in these precise terms, the bishops of Durham were 'prince-bishops', the word 'prince' being used here to denote a supreme ruler. William's attempt to install what we would now call a prince-bishop near the northerly margin of his new kingdom led at first to a spectacular tragedy.

Durham became an important religious centre after the miraculously preserved body of St Cuthbert was brought here in 995AD. According to the legend, the cart on which the coffin lay refused to be moved and this, together with a dream granted to one of the monks who attended it, was taken as evidence that the saint wanted to remain at Durham, which was then covered with dense forest.

The first bishop of Durham was Aldhun, who reigned from 995 to 1018. There were four other Anglo-Saxon bishops before William the Conqueror chose the tall, handsome, white-haired and fresh-faced William Walcher to be both earl of Northumbria, and bishop of Durham in 1071.

The immediate prelude to Walcher's appointment was one of the most terrifying and shameful episodes in English history – the so-called Harrying of the North.

In response to a rebellion in the region, the Conqueror adopted a scorched-earth policy, and seems to have been determined to kill as many northern Anglo-Saxons as he could. He also destroyed their settlements, burned their crops and spread salt on the land to render it infertile for decades to come. As a result, starvation followed, and some were even reduced to cannibalism. The devastation was worst in Yorkshire, but it also affected Cheshire, Shropshire, Derbyshire and Staffordshire. William had done his evil work so well that the wastelands he created were still waste seventeen years later, when the Domesday Book was compiled.

It is thought that as many as a hundred thousand people may have died in the Harrying of the North, but William had stopped the northern rebellion: he was now able to put his own followers in positions of power over the northern lands he had depopulated and laid waste.

The City of Durham saw its own rebellion in February 1069, when Robert Cumin, whom King William had appointed earl of Northumbria, lodged in the city with seven hundred men. It is clear that Cumin had no desire to limit the excesses of his little army, and they treated the Durhamites very cruelly, having already committed what the chronicler Simeon of Durham calls 'ravagings and murders'.

Aethelwin, the last Anglo-Saxon bishop of Durham, and at that time an ally of the Normans, warned Cumin that he was not safe in the city, but the earl ignored him. The bishop was proved right when the local Anglo-Saxons staged a dawn raid, breaking in 'through all the gates' and slaughtering Cumin's followers. It is said that every street ran with blood, and was choked with dead bodies.

Cumin's soldiers made a desperate last stand around the house where the earl was lodged, but the attackers adopted a procedure that was then very popular in such situations: they burned the house down. Simeon tells us there was only one survivor, and this was not the earl.

The Conqueror marched on Durham, intending to revenge the death of his appointee, but a thick mist descended and his force couldn't see their way. Thwarted by the fog, which some said St Cuthbert himself had sent, William turned back. A modern Durham legend has it that this mist appeared again in the summer of 1943, and prevented German bombers from devastating the city.

Cuthbert's influence frustrated the Conqueror again when he visited Durham soon after his appointee Walcher had become both earl of Northumbria and bishop of Durham. Believing, perhaps, that an Anglo-Saxon saint couldn't be all he was cracked up to be, William insisted on seeing Cuthbert's remains. This couldn't happen without some sort of ceremony, and as this unfolded, the king was attacked by a violent fever. Panicked, he rushed out of the church, jumped onto his horse and, so the story goes, didn't stop his horse galloping until he reached the Tees.

William was not, it seems, permanently chastened by this experience, and he soon sent Ralph, one of his agents, to see how much money the king could extract from Durham by way of tribute. St Cuthbert stepped in again and, appearing to Ralph in a dream, proceeded to beat him soundly with his pastoral staff. Ralph woke up feeling very weak, and continued to be ill until he left the bishop's lands.

The Durham Walcher knew was dominated by an Anglo-Saxon church (called the White Church) which had been completed in 1017, which meant that it was less than sixty years old at the time of the Conquest. When Robert Cumin was being burned to death, the flames threatened part of the White Church, but the prayers of the people, together with Cuthbert's influence, drove the flames away. The White Church was cruciform in shape like the later cathedral, and had two towers topped with brass pinnacles, one over the choir and one at the west end. The church stood to the south of the present-day cathedral.

Then as now, the church shared its rocky eminence with a castle, which remained the city residence of the bishops of Durham until the 1830s. The peninsular was defended by walls, surviving parts of which can still be seen here and there in the city. The North and South Baileys are so named because they follow the line of the city's ancient defences. Walcher's castle at Durham was not as welcoming then as it is now – archaeology has revealed that the moat was at least nineteen yards wide and six yards deep.

The remains of St Cuthbert rested in the White Church, attended by a religious community which seems to have consisted of monks and priests of an unusual type, some of whom were married and had children. Archaeology at Durham has found the burials of men, women and children with the characteristic long skulls of the Anglo-Saxons: these burials lay under those of the round-headed Norman monks. The Norman monks were supposed to be celibate, and they formed the community of St Cuthbert after the original, mixed community had been dissolved.

Walcher wanted to get rid of what he may have regarded as the anomalous community that was attached to the White Church, and to replace them with 'proper' monks. To this end, he invited a community of monks that had been established by one Aldwin at Newcastle, to move into the ruins of the old monasteries at Jarrow and Wearmouth. It seems that the first Norman prince-bishop planned to move these monks to Durham and to join their order himself at some point, but his own untimely death frustrated his plans.

Walcher's reputation as a holy man suffered because his followers continued to abuse the local Anglo-Saxon population. Either he was unable to control them, or neglected to do so. In any case, things came to a head when Ligulf, a popular land-owner who also acted as an adviser to the bishop, was murdered by Gilbert, Walcher's deputy as secular ruler of Northumbria.

The murder was planned by Walcher's chaplain, Leobwin, who was also dean of Durham. Leobwin didn't like the way the bishop sometimes followed Ligulf's advice, and not his own. He approached Gilbert, who marched on Ligulf's house with a force of his own followers, combined with some of Leobwin's, and some of Walcher's. Ligulf was slaughtered in his own home, together with almost all of his family.

When Walcher heard of this, he resorted to an ancient demonstration of grief and tore at his clothes: in this case he tore the hood right off his garment. He then informed Leobwin that by his actions he had doomed all of them. He fled to the castle, and sent out messengers with the information that he had had nothing to do with the murder of Ligulf.

Walcher hoped to clear the air over this incident by attending a meeting at nearby Gateshead. It was clear soon after his arrival, however, that the friends of Ligulf who had assembled there in large numbers didn't want to do much talking. Walcher's party fled into the church, hoping to come to some agreement there, but soon all his followers who had remained outside were killed by the mob. Walcher sent Gilbert out, and he was killed. When the bishop himself appeared, he was also killed and then, using the tactic that had been used against Cumin, the mob set fire to the church, and killed the people who rushed out to escape the flames.

The rioters invaded Durham again, much as they had done before the death of Robert Cumin, but Walcher's men managed to fight them off. The king attempted to avenge the death of Walcher by sending his half-brother, our friend Bishop Odo of Bayeux, to lay waste to the whole area. According to Simeon of Durham, many innocent people died, and others were forced to pay money to be spared from this rough justice. With his own men quartered in the castle, Odo set about stripping the White Church of many of its treasures, including a pastoral staff supposed to have been made entirely of sapphire.

Let's Build a Cathedral : William of St Carileph (1081-1096)

The name William was extremely common among the Normans and their allies from the other side of the English Channel. It is no surprise, then, that the bishop of Durham who followed William Walcher was also called William, or that he remained as bishop under two kings called William.

William of St Carileph (or William of St Calais) was a protégé of Odo, the aforementioned bishop of Bayeux. He was certainly part of the chapter at Bayeux when Odo was bishop, but later, like his father before him, Carileph became a Benedictine monk at the abbey of St Calais in Maine. He later rose to become abbot of St Vincent-des-Prés, outside the walls of Le Mans.

Given his background as a Benedictine monk, it is hardly surprising that Carileph should have completed Walcher's plan and installed monks of that order at Durham. This was a big step, and Carileph made sure that he had the approval of the archbishop of Canterbury, and King William and his queen, Matilda, before he proceeded. The Conqueror even sent Carileph to Rome to get the approval of Pope Gregory VII.

The monks who took over from the old, irregular community of St Cuthbert were imported by Carileph from the monasteries at Jarrow and Wearmouth, which had been re-founded by William Walcher.

Carileph was careful to make the new Benedictine priory at Durham independent from his bishopric, and indeed it was supported for centuries by its own lands. Thus began the division of the rock on which Durham cathedral and the castle stand into two distinct zones: a monastic area to the south of the church, and an area controlled by the bishop to the north, where the castle stands. Good fences, they say, make good neighbours.

Carileph seems to have thrived under William the Conqueror, and may even have had an important role in the organisation of William's great survey of his new kingdom – the Domesday Book. But in 1087 the Conqueror died at Caen in France, and Carileph had severe problems with his successor, William II, known as

William Rufus.

The Conqueror had ruled both Normandy and England, but at his death he bequeathed Normandy to his oldest son, Robert Curthose, and England to William Rufus, his second oldest surviving son. This arrangement caused problems in England, because quite a lot of the Norman hierarchy would have preferred to be ruled by Robert. These malcontents included Odo, bishop of Bayeux. According to the twelfth century chronicler William of Malmesbury, Odo also resented the power Carileph enjoyed under the new king. This was the sort of power Odo himself had exercised under William the Conqueror until he was imprisoned by that monarch (for reasons that are unclear) in the early 1080s.

According to Simeon of Durham's *History of the kings of England*, Odo led a rebellion against Rufus, and was joined in this by the majority of the new Norman aristocracy of England. An important ally of Rufus at this time was Lanfranc, the archbishop of Canterbury.

William Rufus replied to this Norman rebellion with a force of English, or Anglo-Saxons, who managed to stop the rebels in their tracks, and to force Odo to leave England for Normandy. Carileph came under suspicion because, when he had been riding with the king into Sussex and Kent during the rebellion, he had withdrawn, promising to return with more forces. He never returned, and this made William Rufus think that he had been one of the conspirators.

In March 1088 Carileph's lands were confiscated, and in November of the same year he was brought before the king and Lanfranc at a sort of tribunal at Old Sarum near Salisbury. Here Carileph pleaded that he had done nothing wrong, and that in any case, as a bishop, he could only be tried in an ecclesiastical court. Those on the side of the king and Lanfranc argued that he was not being tried as a bishop, but as a baron with secular power over large areas of land. Carileph's opponents were, therefore, by a sort of legal fiction, trying to separate him into two people - a bishop and a landlord.

At last Carileph was granted safe passage to Normandy with 'his people, with their goods', including 'gold and silver, horses and clothes, and arms, and dogs, and hawks, and anything which they ought to carry from the land'.

In February 1091 William Rufus invaded Normandy and, during the siege of a castle held by the English king's forces, Carileph managed to negotiate a truce. Soon there was a larger truce between Rufus and his brother Robert Curthose, duke of Normandy and, all being forgiven, Carileph was allowed to return to Durham.

William was now over sixty, a good ripe age for a man living in eleventh-century Europe. Given his past travels, his political problems, and the hard work he had put into reforming the monastic community at Durham, we might have expected him to regard this last period in the north as a time for retirement and reflection. Instead, the bishop set about one of the most ambitious schemes ever conceived by a bishop of any nation – the building of the greatest cathedral in the world.

Visitors to Durham are usually impressed by the size and age of the cathedral, and some no doubt wonder how such a huge and beautiful building could have been built, or even conceived of, in the eleventh century, when technology was so primitive. Part of the secret is to do with the availability of much cheap labour. Some work would have been done, in effect, for free, as many of the tenants of the bishops' lands would have been obliged to give their landlord a number of days of work per year, as part of their rent. These unskilled labourers might have been employed on such tasks as shifting large numbers of roughly-dressed stones up the hill to the cathedral site. Almost all the stones used in the cathedral are small enough to be carried by two reasonably healthy people on foot.

The fact that the cathedral stands on a high, steep-sided rock must have presented particular problems, especially when transporting the larger stones, and the pieces of wood used for scaffolding, or as 'centering' when vaulted roofs were being constructed. Ox-carts would probably have been used for this purpose.

The harsh northern winters, felt especially keenly at this

exposed site, might have made construction work impossible, so that during the colder months the masons may have worked under shelter, dressing stones ready for the resumption of building in the spring.

At times there would probably have been over four hundred people working at the cathedral site, all of whom would have to have got there from somewhere, and all of whom would need food and drink. Workers brought in from elsewhere would also have needed accommodation within walking distance. Many of them would have ended their working day with pale yellow stone dust in every fibre of their woollen clothes, in every pore and wrinkle of their skin, and coating every hair on their heads, and in their beards.

Many skilled, specialist workers and craftsmen were employed building the great Norman cathedrals of England, some of whom would have been imported from the Continent.

The Anglo-Saxon White Church Carileph had inherited had been completed less than eighty years before the bishop decided to demolish it, but it seems that, despite its newness, its two towers and its brass pinnacles, it couldn't compare with the fine buildings Carileph had seen in France, and on his journey to Rome.

Since the plan of the new building was to be in the shape of a Latin cross, it is clear from the height and length of the walls of the choir, which was built while Carileph was still alive, that the bishop intended to build something as long as the cathedral is now, minus the Galilee Chapel and the Chapel of the Nine Altars, which were both added later. Carileph re-used stone from the White Church, and got more from local quarries at Kepier, Baxter Wood and Littleburn. This was the pale yellow sandstone of the Durham Coal Levels, a material so widespread in parts of County Durham that quarries were once found all over the place.

While the cathedral was being built, the monks were putting up their own buildings, getting some of their stone from the nearby Sacrist's Quarry, near Prebends Bridge in Durham City. As building work progressed, St Cuthbert himself lay in the cloisters, where a gilded effigy of him was erected, which stood there until the Reformation.

The foundation stone of the new cathedral was laid on the eleventh of August 1093, in a ceremony attended by Carileph, Turgot the prior of Durham and the Scottish king Malcolm Canmore (meaning 'Malcolm Bighead'). Malcolm, who was to die later that year, was the same Malcolm who is declared king of Scotland at the end of Shakespeare's play, *Macbeth*. If Carileph intended his invitation to Malcolm as a peace offering for the Scottish king, who represented a military threat to the north of England, then his gesture was later ruined by the king of England. Malcolm was in Durham on his way to meet William at Gloucester, but when he got there the king refused to see him at all. On his return to his own kingdom Malcolm organised a punitive invasion of the north country, but was ambushed and killed by Robert de Mowbray, the earl of Northumbria.

Carileph's ambitions for his new home for the bones of St Cuthbert suggest not only that the Church at Durham was rich, but also that the bishop felt that its income would continue to be good, and that peace between England and Scotland, and within England itself, would prevail long enough to allow for the completion of such a project.

Building started at the east end and marched west. By the time Carileph died in 1096, the choir had been completed, though it still lacked its roof of stone vaulting.

Despite his wealth, his achievements and the fact that he had survived some major upheavals in his life, Carileph seems to have died a very depressed man. Three years before, one of his knights had lain, apparently dead, for three days, but had awoken, like a Norman Dante, to tell the tale of his visit to hell. There he had seen, among other things, his master William of St Carileph dwelling for eternity in the midst of a 'horrid wilderness', in a grim building constructed entirely of iron. Such prophecies were taken very seriously in those days.

Carileph collapsed on Christmas day 1095 at Windsor, and died on the morning of January the second. He was buried in the Chapter House at Durham.

A Bishop in the Tower: Ranulf Flambard (1099-1128)

Although he made peace with Carileph, and restored him to his see, it is clear that William Rufus didn't always trust the bishop of Durham he had inherited on the death of his father. When Carileph died, Rufus appointed one of his own closest advisers, a man he had raised up from a lowly social position, and someone he no doubt believed he could trust. Unfortunately, almost everyone else thought that Ranulf Flambard, the king's chaplain, was not to be trusted at all.

According to William of Malmesbury, Ranulf was the 'inciter' of the king's 'covetousness', always dreaming up new ways to exact money from the English. In fact, one of Flambard's roles was *exactor*, charged with filling Rufus's pockets. Malmesbury tells us that Ranulf the *exactor* automatically doubled any tribute that was granted to the king. He also encouraged Rufus to leave valuable clerical posts empty for a long time after the previous occupants died, and to keep the income for himself.

Flambard was tall and handsome, though rather fat in later life, and seems to have possessed the ability to take command of any situation, and get the better of anyone, even in exalted company. He could feign anger by frowning and raising his voice, and he would also interlard his speech with such a stream of jokes that people couldn't tell whether or not he was being serious.

As he gathered ill-gotten riches for his master, Flambard could hardly help becoming rich in his own right. It is thought that he may even have been able to buy the see of Durham from William Rufus for £1000. He was consecrated in June 1099, but a little over a year later, in August 1100, William Rufus was killed in a hunting accident in the New Forest. Given the king's lack of popularity, and the fact that many of his nobles thought he should never have been king in the first place, there has always been speculation that the 'hunting accident' was actually a planned assassination.

William Rufus was succeeded by his brother, Henry, who had been present when his brother had been shot 'by accident' with an arrow. One of Henry's first actions as king was to arrest the newly-minted bishop of Durham. In fact, it took Henry less than two weeks to put Ranulf in chains. The bishop became the first state prisoner to be locked up in the Tower of London: after six months, he became the first to escape from the Tower. As we shall see, Flambard was not the last bishop of Durham to be arrested and imprisoned; nor was he the last to be kept in the Tower. Writing in the *Durham University Journal* in the early 1970s, H.S. Offler called Flambard's 1101 escape 'pure Gilbert and Sullivan'.

Flambard's butler sent in a flagon of wine for his master. The bishop used this to get his guards drunk. He then pulled out the rope that had been hidden in the bottom of the flagon and, having attached it to part of the window, started to climb down the rope.

Ranulf was probably about forty years old at this time, and rather fat. He had no gloves, though gloves were supposed to be part of his outfit as a bishop.

He was doing quite well until he reached the end of the rope, when he realised he still had some way to go before he reached the ground. His palms burned from the rope, and badly shaken by his fall, he met up with some friends who were waiting for him by prior arrangement. They rode to the coast, and soon Flambard was in Normandy – clearly the bolt-hole of choice for the aristocracy of Norman England. The keeper of the Tower, one William de Mandeville, was heavily fined after this embarrassing mistake.

The escape from the Tower might seem like an outlandish escapade for a corpulent, middle-aged bishop, but even before he was elevated to the see of Durham, Flambard had experienced an even more exciting adventure. He had been kidnapped and taken out to sea by a confederation of his enemies, led by one Gerold. As soon as he realised what was happening, Flambard threw his seal-ring and seal overboard, so that these could not be used by his kidnappers to seal fraudulent documents.

On board, two 'sons of Belial' argued over whether they should throw Ranulf overboard or beat out his brains. For their pay, they were to have Ranulf's clothes, but they soon started arguing over who should get which item. Meanwhile a storm blew up and drove the ship back onto the coast. Taking advantage of some hesitation he sensed among the sailors, the future bishop of Durham used his smooth tongue to secure his release.

The corpulence that had hindered his escape from the Tower was not the only result of Ranulf Flambard's various appetites. He had a number of children who, like some of his other relatives, he managed to get into powerful jobs on both sides of the Channel. Thanks to Flambard's influence, his son Thomas became bishop of Lisieux, although he was under twelve years old at the time. This ludicrous appointment meant that Ranulf could act as guardian and live on the proceeds of Lisieux while he remained in exile.

Before he became a bishop, Flambard had a relationship with an English woman called Ælgifu, who may even have been his wife and the mother of some or all of his children. Ælgifu later married another man in Huntingdon, her home town, and Ranulf used to stay with this couple on his frequent trips down to London. On one of these stopovers the bishop, who was by now in his mid fifties, tried to seduce the teenage niece of Ælgifu's husband. On this occasion, Ranulf's looks, his quick wits and his powers of persuasion all failed him. The girl managed to lock him in his room, with herself on the outside.

In Normandy, Flambard acted as an adviser to Robert Curthose, and accompanied him when he attempted to invade England in 1101. This invasion came to nothing, but Henry and Robert were reconciled, and Durham was eventually restored to Flambard.

According to Simeon's Continuator, the newly-returned bishop set about squeezing as much income as he could from the lands that had been restored to him. Although his predecessor, William of St Carileph, had secured the financial independence of the priory at Durham, Flambard did not respect this, and made free with the monks' money, using it to finance projects of his own.

As it happened, at least two of Flambard's projects were extremely worthy, and they suggest that, despite his history of sharp practice, he was trying to secure for himself a respectable legacy. He continued the building of Carileph's cathedral, though progress went on by fits and starts as the money available went up and down. Flambard also built Framwellgate Bridge over the River

Wear in Durham.

About a month before his death, Flambard was carried into the unfinished cathedral and, seated facing the altar, heaved a great sigh. He then repented openly that he had robbed the church of a great deal of money, and trampled over its ancient freedoms and privileges. As a visible sign that he was paying his debts and restoring his see to the condition in which he had found it, he took off his ring and laid it on the altar. His determination to do right by Durham before his death was reflected in two special charters.

Ranulf Flambard was buried in the Chapter House at Durham, and when his bones were unveiled in 1874, it was determined that he had probably been about five feet and nine inches tall, with a strong lower jaw and a somewhat elongated head.

After the death of Flambard, the see was vacant for nearly five years, during which time it was controlled by two barons. During this period the nave of the cathedral was finished.

Odo, William I and Robert Curthose

Seal of Hugh du Puiset

Seal of Anthony Bek as Patriarch of Jerusalem

John Cosin (top) and his Nemesis, Peter Smart

Auckland Castle

Killed by Pancake Day: Hugh du Puiset (1153-1195)

The new cathedral not only separated the domain of the Durham monks from the domain of the bishop. It also separated monks and clergy from lay worshippers, and men from women.

During services, the monks assembled in the choir, while male members of the public stood in the nave. Women were restricted to the portion of the nave that lay beyond what is now the main public entrance to the cathedral. Visitors can still see the line of grey stones set into the floor, beyond which women were not meant to stray. This unusual arrangement was supposed to be in place because St Cuthbert was thought to dislike women – an accusation that has no firm basis in the story of Cuthbert's life. It may be that the cathedral authorities didn't want women to get too near the monks, who were, of course, supposed to be celibate.

Hugh du Puiset, the seventh bishop after the Conquest, is thought to have built the Galilee Chapel onto the west end of the nave so as to give female worshippers a special place of their own in the cathedral. Like Ranulf Flambard, Puiset had had rather more to do with women than a bishop of that time was supposed to have had, and may have had as many as four sons by his mistress, Alice de Percy. Like Flambard, he sought and found elevated positions for his offspring – one of his sons, named Burchard, became archdeacon of Durham.

The Galilee is a Lady Chapel, dedicated to the Virgin Mary, and Lady chapels are usually built at the east end of a cathedral or church. When Puiset began to build his Lady Chapel at the east end, the walls started to sag and crack. This was not blamed on inadequate foundations, but on the intervention of St Cuthbert who, it was thought, would not have liked women worshippers so near his tomb.

The Galilee, Puiset's greatest contribution to the architecture of the cathedral, might be said to reflect his own personality. It is magnificent but rather relentless, with its zig-zags running all round the semi-circular arches. It is nowhere near as substantial-looking as the interior of the nave, and it is also rather cold.

Visitors must try to picture how it must have looked when it was painted all over inside – the surviving wall-paintings in the Galilee make this easier to imagine.

The Galilee reflects not just the taste of Bishop du Puiset – it also stands as a monument to his extravagance. Local stone was not good enough for him and he sent abroad – probably to Normandy – for the stone for his Lady Chapel. He also had extravagant taste in priestly vestments. According to G.V. Scammell, who published a biography of Puiset in 1956, the bishop owned a red velvet chasuble embroidered 'in gold and bezants, and studded with great pearls and precious stones, whilst another was in black, emblazoned with a bizarre assortment of jewels, golden stars and griffons'.

When Puiset was planning to join the Third Crusade with King Richard I in 1189, he assembled a fleet of ships for himself, one of which was so large that it needed a crew of thirty-two to sail it. Some of the domestic equipment specially made for this ship included silver pots and pans, and it was also to carry an ornate silver throne. In the end, King Richard forbade Puiset to go on crusade with him, but he did take his ships.

Richard I appointed Puiset as one of the two 'justiciars', charged with running the country while the king was away on crusade. For a short time in December 1189 Puiset ruled England alone from Windsor while his fellow justiciar, the chancellor William de Longchamps, was in France with the king. By April 1190 King Richard had demoted Puiset to the inferior position of justiciar of the north. This was one of many disappointments and humiliations suffered by Puiset in the fields of national and international politics.

The bishop of Durham was not a man to take kindly to having William de Longchamps, who was bishop of Ely as well as chancellor, set above him. When Longchamps strayed into Puiset's 'patch' by visiting York on official business in May 1190, Puiset was seriously offended. He confronted Longchamps at Blyth and, according to Scammell, 'greeted him with mistimed arrogance'. When the two men met the following week, Longchamps, whose power in the land Puiset had underestimated, arrested the bishop of Durham and placed him under house arrest at Howden in Yorkshire. It wasn't until the fifth of August that the king ordered his release.

Richard I, known as the Lionheart, was generally pretty good for Puiset's career, and in 1189 he even allowed him to buy the earldom of Northumberland for the promise of two thousand marks. When Puiset donned the ring and shield that symbolised his possession of this earldom, the king remarked that he had made a young earl out of an old bishop.

Hugh du Puiset was so attached to the magnificent treasures of Durham Cathedral, many of which he himself had paid for, that he declined to give them up in part-payment of the king's ransom, when Richard I was imprisoned by Emperor Henry VI at Trifels castle in south-west Germany. Instead the bishop sent £2000, which did not please Richard at all.

Puiset showed his support for Richard in 1194 by assembling 'a great army drawn from Yorkshire, Northumberland and his own lands, and lavishly equipped with siege engines' to lay siege to the castle of Tickhill, which belonged to the king's brother John. When the castle surrendered and Puiset met the king at Nottingham, he could not have been higher in the Lionheart's favour. Typically, he offended Richard within a month by upsetting his friend, the king of Scotland, in a petty argument over the right to use a hunting lodge at Brackley.

Puiset seems to have had a talent for offending people who were more powerful than he was. He also offended the monks of his own cathedral, but he could offend them without getting himself into too much trouble. Like Ranulf Flambard, Puiset ignored the independence granted to the monks by William of St Carileph, and at one stage he may have managed to take all their rights and privileges into his own hands. The monks responded by producing documents which proved their rights, many of which documents are now known to have been forged.

Puiset died at Howden in 1195, having previously endangered his health by eating too much on Shrove Tuesday at Crayke. He was about seventy years old, and had been bishop of Durham for forty-two years. His reign was long enough for him to have served under nine popes and three different kings of England – Stephen, Henry II and Richard I. When he was first elected under King Stephen, who was his uncle, he no doubt expected to be an important player, both nationally and internationally, but Stephen died shortly after Puiset's election. We have already seen how Puiset blundered in and out of Richard's favour – he aroused the suspicions of Henry II by appearing to side with his rebellious son, and allowing a Scottish army to march through Durham unhindered.

Given the immense wealth and power the see of Durham brought him, it is perhaps surprising that Puiset didn't just stay at home and enjoy what he had, instead of jostling for more power with dangerous characters like William de Longchamps. It is not as if he didn't know what he possessed in the north-east. In 1183 he commissioned a survey of his lands, which historians now call the Boldon Book. This includes information on the money and service owed to the bishop by his tenants, great and small. The Boldon Book is a useful adjunct to the Domesday Book, which was compiled nearly a century earlier. Domesday doesn't cover any land north-east of the Tees, perhaps because the country was so chaotic and lawless that the Domesday commissioners just didn't want to risk trying to do a survey there.

The Boldon Book tells us, for instance, that Reginald the Fuller of Durham paid three shillings a year for land rented from the bishop. The land occupied by one Lefwine 'across the river next to the meadow' yielded sixteen pence, whereas his neighbour Walrann paid only half that amount. The retired Abbot of Peterborough, living at Newton near Durham, paid one mark for land previously occupied by Richard the Engineer – perhaps a man employed at a high level on building work for the bishop or the prior.

A War of Attrition: Anthony Bek (1283-1311)

The official business at York that William de Longchamps was engaged in in 1190 was to do with the aftermath of another shameful episode in English history – the massacre of as many as one hundred and fifty Jews in that city, in the same year. King Richard's instruction to Lonchamps on this occasion was to be as harsh with the perpetrators, some of whom were associates of du Puiset, as he could.

Although some Jews may have come to Britain in Roman times, it was the Normans who first brought significant numbers into England. Monarchs like Richard I valued them for their expertise in financial matters, but anti-semitism continued, and in 1290, Edward I ordered all Jews out of England.

Like most medieval kings, Edward still needed money, especially since he felt the need to fight wars against the Welsh and the Scots. Unable to borrow from the Jews he had expelled, the king was forced to make deals with Italian bankers and continental merchants.

Bek, who was probably born around 1245, was of an age with Edward, and had accompanied Lord Edward, as he then was, on crusade before he became king in 1272. At Acre, in what is now Israel, the future king had survived an assassination attempt but was left with a nasty stab-wound, which became infected in the summer heat. A brave doctor offered to perform an operation – without anaesthetic, of course – during which he planned to trim off all the infected flesh. Given the poor success rates of medieval surgery, Edward was wise to choose eight of his companions to act as administrators if both he and his father Henry III were to die while Edward's heir was still a minor. One of the eight was Anthony Bek, Oxford graduate, future bishop of Durham and son of a land-owning knight based at Eresby in Lincolnshire.

When Edward, now recovered, became king, Bek became his right-hand man, performing every kind of high-level job for him, including arranging loans, participating in legal cases and matchmaking in dynastic marriages. Nicholas Harris Nicolas, in an appendix to Carrick's *Life of Sir William Wallis*, explains that 'scarcely a single event of any importance took place during the reign of Edward the First...but in which he [Bek] was concerned'.

Bek drew a salary of £100 a year as secretary to the king, but he also assembled various other incomes, particularly from ecclesiastical jobs that he held 'in plurality', so that he could not be expected to actually work at all of them. This 'pluralism', which gave Bek money for work he wasn't really expected to do, was frowned on by the papacy at this time, as it was a sign of weakness and corruption in the Church. Among the various ecclesiastical positions Bek held before he was made bishop of Durham was that of archdeacon of Durham.

Bek was elected as bishop after a time of great conflict both for the monks and the bishop of Durham. When Bek's immediate predecessor as bishop, Robert of Holy Island, died in 1283, the conflict showed no sign of going away. The monks of Durham were locked in a bitter dispute with William Wickwane, the archbishop of York. Wickwane regarded himself as the direct superior of any bishop of Durham, and claimed the right to make an official visit – called a Visitation – of Durham cathedral, the bishop of Durham and the monks of Durham.

When Wickwane attempted to make his Visitation in the summer of 1281 he was seen as a threat to the independence of the church at Durham, and was driven out of the convent. This was only one episode in a protracted dispute between Durham and York, and both sides appealed to Pope Martin IV.

The Durham monks also showed their independence in 1283, when the king asked them to lend him some money they had collected in the name of the pope, which was supposed to be used to finance a crusade. This request was repeated by Anthony Bek, on behalf of the king, in his early days as bishop, but before he had been formally enthroned in the cathedral. The monks resorted to classic delaying tactics over the payment of the money and it became clear that Richard de Hoton, the subprior, was a ringleader in this resistance.

When Anthony Bek was enthroned in the cathedral on

29

Christmas Eve 1285 he took the opportunity to show the archbishop of York and the monks of the Durham that he was not a man to be trifled with. He refused to be enthroned by a representative of the archbishop or by Richard de Claxton, the prior of Durham. Instead, the ceremony of enthronement was carried out by Anthony's own brother Thomas, who was bishop of St David's in Wales.

By this time the Chapel of the Nine Altars had been built as a magnificent extension to the east end of the cathedral. Three days after his enthronement the new bishop held a closed meeting in the chapel, which had been completed only eleven years earlier. There he planned his next step in the company of his brother Thomas and some senior local monks. The prior and subprior of Durham were not included in this conversation.

There was then a procession into the chapter house, where Thomas Bek calmly announced that the prior now had permission to leave his post, since he had declared himself too ill to continue, and had handed in his resignation. This was a surprise to most of the monks, and not least to Prior Claxton, who had not tendered any resignation to anybody. The subprior, the fiery Richard de Hoton, raised several objections, but when the elderly Hugh de Derlington came out of retirement to become prior for the second time in 1286, he banished Hoton to a tiny branch (or 'cell') of the Durham convent at Lytham in Lancashire.

While he was bishop of Durham, Anthony Bek continued to serve the king. In 1296 Bek joined King Edward in a campaign against the Scots, bringing with him five hundred horsemen and fifteen hundred foot-soldiers. During this campaign, the Scots lost a battle at Dunbar because they foolishly came down from their strong defensive position to fight on the plain. The same was to happen over three hundred and fifty years later, when a Scottish army lost at Dunbar to Oliver Cromwell.

On the tenth of July 1296 King John of Scotland surrendered to Anthony Bek at Brechin – on this occasion the bishop was standing in for the king of England as he had done many times before in Britain and on the Continent. Two years later Bek assisted Edward again in another war against the Scots, who were led this time by the famous William Wallace. During this campaign, Bek captured the strategically important castle of Dirleton, between Edinburgh and Dunbar.

Meanwhile back in Durham, Richard de Hoton had returned from exile and was elected prior in 1290. There seems to have been peace between Hoton and Bek for ten years, but in May 1300 the bishop announced his intention to conduct a Visitation of the cathedral priory, to investigate complaints against Hoton's administration. This announcement started a legal war of attrition between Hoton and Bek that was to last until Hoton's death, eight years later.

The low point of this conflict happened near the beginning, when Bek excommunicated Hoton and blockaded the monastery for over three months. Nothing and nobody could get in or out – even deliveries of food were blocked and in the hot, dry month of August the convent's water supply was cut off. Also in August, the convent was stormed and Hoton was dragged into a prison cell by monks loyal to Bek. In the following December, Hoton escaped and went on to present his case to both the king of England and the pope.

The dispute with Hoton meant that Bek himself had to travel to Rome to consult with the pope, and Pope Clement V was so impressed with the bishop of Durham that he gave him the title of patriarch of Jerusalem. This was an empty title, since Jerusalem was in the hands of the Muslims at that time, but it did make Bek the senior churchman in England. He was also given the job of heading an investigation into the Knights Templar in the British Isles – this order of knights was suppressed in 1312, the year after Bek's death.

Bek's challenge to the Durham convent was part of his strategy of maximising his power over the traditional land of the prince-bishops – between Tyne and Tees. His attempt to become, in effect, king of an autonomous region within England brought him into conflict with his old friend Edward I. Edward seized Durham from its bishop twice – Bek was only restored to his place after the death of Edward I and the accession of his son Edward II. The second Edward seems to have regarded Bek as something like a generous and affectionate uncle, who had at times made peace between his father and himself.

In the end, Bek won out over his opponents by dint of sheer persistence, and by cleverly outliving his enemies. The long-awaited Visitation of the Durham convent took place in February 1309. At this time Hoton's successor, Prior William de Tanfield, gave up all legal claims against the bishop.

Bek died in March 1311 and became the first man after St Cuthbert himself to be buried in Durham cathedral – the usual place of burial for the bishops was the chapter house.

The Golden Old Man: Cuthbert Tunstall (1530-1559)

We have seen how Bishop Flambard was imprisoned in the Tower of London, and how Anthony Bek was deprived of his bishopric - twice. Cuthbert Tunstall, who was bishop of Durham at the time of the English Reformation, was also imprisoned in the Tower and also twice deprived of his bishopric.

Like du Puiset, Tunstall came from an aristocratic family and, like Bek, he was employed at the highest level in the government of England, both at home and on the Continent. Like Bek, Tunstall was an Oxford graduate, but Tunstall was also educated at Cambridge, and at the University of Padua in Italy. Tunstall was so well-regarded as a scholar that he was a close and valued friend of both Erasmus and Thomas More.

Before he became bishop of Durham, Tunstall found himself right into the middle of the events that led up to Henry VIII's split with Rome, events that ultimately transformed England into a Protestant country. When he was still bishop of London, Tunstall was chosen as a member of the defence team for Katherine of Aragon, the first wife of King Henry. The king had convinced himself that his marriage to Katherine was cursed because she had previously been married to his deceased older brother, Arthur.

Marriages between brothers-in-law and sisters-in-law were supposed to be forbidden in the Old Testament book of Leviticus. Katherine's case was that she had never been properly married to Arthur, as their marriage had never been consummated. At first Tunstall, who remained a conservative Catholic all his life, agreed with Katherine, but he eventually defected from the queen's side and supported Henry.

It may be that Tunstall was given Durham because he had shown his loyalty to the king by turning against Katherine, but it is more likely that, as a determined, popular and well-respected Catholic, the king wanted Tunstall out of the way while he abandoned his queen and took personal control of the Church in England.

Among the important local events that effected Tunstall as bishop of Durham was the Pilgrimage of Grace, a series of rebellions, effecting mainly the north of England, against the religious and financial changes that Henry was introducing. When news of the rebellion reached him in his castle at Bishop Auckland, Tunstall fled to another castle at Norham, so that when as many as ten thousand rebels (or 'pilgrims') looted Auckland Castle, the bishop wasn't there. The pilgrims then went on to sack the chancery at Durham.

The effects of the Reformation on Tunstall's position as prince-bishop, and also on Durham cathedral itself, were unprecedented. When Tunstall became bishop of Durham in 1530 he was still able to rule virtually as a king, but when the Resumption Act of April 1536 came into force, the judicial powers of the bishop of Durham were seized by the Crown. Before this, the bishop had complete control over the administration of justice in his own territory, and crimes were breaches not of the king's peace, but of the bishop's. At around this time, the bishop of Durham also stopped minting his own coins.

The cult of St Cuthbert, centred on his sacred relics, was not consistent with the new Protestant atmosphere. According to *The rites of Durham*, a valuable source on the cathedral before the Reformation, Cuthbert was housed in a shrine 'exalted with most curious workmanship in fine and costly marble, all limned and gilded with gold'. In 1537 or 1538 a group of official Visitors appointed by Henry VIII demolished the shrine and broke open the saint's coffin with a sledge-hammer. Apparently the blow was so forceful that one of Cuthbert's legs was broken.

After eight hundred years, Cuthbert's body was found to be complete, except for the tip of the nose. He was wearing a sapphire ring, and the cloths he was wrapped in seemed remarkably fresh. The body was removed to the vestry, where it remained for some years until Tunstall had it buried in a new coffin, not in an exalted shrine, but below the pavement of the cathedral, where it still rests today.

Catholic tradition has it that the body that lies behind the altar at Durham today is not that of Cuthbert at all, and that his real body was stolen away so that it would not rest in a Protestant cathedral.

Durham Abbey was dissolved at the end of 1539, and Prior Whitehead, the last leader of the monks, became Dean Whitehead. He was succeeded by Robert Horne, who proceeded with the work of 'Protestantising' the cathedral by smashing much of the stained glass and removing the golden effigy of St Cuthbert that stood in the cloisters, on the site where the saint's bones had rested while the cathedral was being built.

By this time Henry VIII had died and been replaced by his son Edward VI, whose mother was the old king's third wife, Jane Seymour. Edward was only nine when he came to the throne in 1547, and during his short reign the country was dominated first by his uncle the duke of Somerset, and later by John Dudley, duke of Northumberland. It was thanks to Dudley that Bishop Tunstall ended up in the Tower of London, having been found guilty of concealing a plot – presumably a plot against Dudley himself.

When the sickly King Edward died in 1553 at the tender age of fifteen, his half-sister Mary became queen. Mary was determined to re-convert England to Catholicism, and during her reign the well-know Catholic bishop of Durham was released from captivity and restored to his see. Mary earned her nickname 'Bloody Mary' by beginning a horrific program of persecuting Protestants, many of whom were burned at the stake. Although he participated in the trials of some leading Protestants, Tunstall didn't sentence any of them to death, though in a rare flash of anger he called Bishop John Hooper a 'beast' when he admitted that he was married.

Hooper was also criticised by Tunstall because of his beliefs about the bread given out during communion. Unlike Tunstall, Hooper did not believe that the bread actually became the body of Christ. The bishop of Durham was particularly strong in his beliefs about the communion bread, and also keen that priests should not marry. Dean Robert Horne of Durham is supposed to have brought his wife into the parts of the cathedral where women had previously been forbidden, and this was one reason why he fled abroad during Mary's reign.

Queen Mary died childless in 1558, at the age of forty-two. She was succeeded by her half-sister Elizabeth, the daughter of Henry VIII by his second wife, Anne Boleyn. Elizabeth, who ruled for forty-five years and became famous as the Virgin Queen, proved to be loyal to the Protestant side of Christianity. Tunstall probably only met her once, during which meeting he openly criticised her religious stance, and advised her to take a more moderate line, like that followed by her father, Henry VIII. According to Quadra, the Spanish ambassador, 'it was all to no avail, and they only laugh[ed] at him'.

Tunstall's second and last period of imprisonment followed his refusal to sign the Act of Supremacy of 1559. This was 'An Act restoring to the Crown the ancient Jurisdiction over the State Ecclesiastical and Spiritual, and abolishing all Foreign Power repugnant to the same' - in other words, the English Church was again breaking off from Rome.

Tunstall was imprisoned this time, not in the Tower, but in the house at Lambeth of the new archbishop of Canterbury, Matthew Parker. There Tunstall spent the last eight weeks of his life, no doubt tolerating the presence of Mrs Parker, and also tolerating Parker's attempts to gently bring him round to the Protestant way of thinking. The moderation shown towards Tunstall at this time

35

was no doubt partly inspired by people's reverence for his old age – he was now eighty-five, an age that few subjects of the first Queen Elizabeth would ever attain.

Tunstall was buried not at Durham but in Lambeth parish church, under a slab of black marble. The slab bore a brass plate inscribed with a poetic Latin epitaph composed by Walter Haddon, who referred to Tunstall as the 'golden old man'.

Picking Up the Pieces: John Cosin (1660-1672)

Cuthbert Tunstall was proud to be called a Catholic, but John Cosin, who became bishop of Durham at the time of the Restoration, always asserted that he was an Anglican, though he was often accused of leaning towards Roman Catholicism.

Cosin, who was a prebendary at Durham long before he was made bishop, had a taste for elaborate ceremony, beautiful church music, and church decorations that looked a little too Catholic for the English Puritans of the time. A Puritan fellow-prebendary at Durham, a man called Peter Smart, preached a sermon against Cosin's liturgical style in 1628. The sermon, which was soon published, painted a lurid picture of Cosin's 'altar decking, cope wearing, organ playing, piping and singing, crossing of cushions and kissing of clouts, oft starting up and squatting down, nodding of heads, and whirling about till their noses stand eastward...'

Cosin was an expert on liturgy, and he could grow tetchy if his services didn't go as he wanted them to. Noticing that a Mrs Heath was not participating in all the 'starting up' required in one of his services, Cosin grabbed at her sleeve (tearing it in the process) and called her a 'lazy sow'.

There was also some concern about the number of candles Cosin liked to have around the cathedral at Candlemas, which suggests that, beyond a certain number, the display would start to look Catholic to Puritan eyes. Peter Smart accused Cosin of busying himself at Candlemas 'from two of the clock in the afternoone till foure, in climbing up long ladders to sticke up wax candles in the Cathedrall Church'. When the dean sent a servant to take down some of these candles during a service, 'Dr Cosin did struggle with him in the time of prayer, to the great disturbance of the congregation'.

Smart insisted that Cosin's followers were 'the Whore of Babylon's dastardly brood...that painted harlot of the Church of Rome'. Such language was vivid even by the standards of the religious controversies of the seventeenth century, and the upshot was that Smart lost his place. He was nothing if not persistent, however, and when he brought a long list of accusations against Cosin before the House of Lords in 1641, Cosin was lucky to escape with his freedom.

By this time Britain was heading for civil war. King Charles I was in Scotland, and Cosin, who was, among other things, Master of Peterhouse College, Cambridge, was found guilty of trying to send money and college plate from Peterhouse to the king. He was ejected from his mastership of Peterhouse in 1644, having already been declared unfit for his position as dean of Peterborough by the House of Commons.

It was not just Cosin's approach to liturgy that made him obnoxious to the Puritans who had so much political power at this time. His writings, the fact that he was respected by the king, and had been employed by bishops (whom some of the Puritans wanted to abolish) made Cosin's position in England untenable. Fearing imprisonment and perhaps even execution, Cosin fled to France disguised, it is said, as a miller.

Cosin's various appointments and benefices at Durham, Cambridge and elsewhere had made him a rich man, but as an exile most of his status and income was lost to him. As the son of a Norwich 'louse-pricker', meaning a tailor or someone in the garment trade, Cosin had no private income to fall back on, and when Charles I was executed in 1649 the future bishop of Durham was reduced to penury.

He became attached to the court of Charles's widowed queen Henrietta Maria in Paris, and served as chaplain to the Protestant members of her circle. He also came to know her son Charles there – the man who already regarded himself as King Charles II, but who would not be properly restored to his throne for over a decade after his father's death.

One legend states that during this time of exile Charles's English mistress, Lucy Walter, gave Cosin a mysterious black box that was not to be opened until the death of Charles II. This was supposed to contain evidence that Charles had actually married Lucy, and that their son the duke of Monmouth was therefore not illegitimate, but was in fact Charles's rightful heir.

Later, when Charles had ruled in England for about a decade, it became clear that his Portuguese queen, Catherine of Braganza, was not likely to produce an heir. In the face of her regular miscarriages, interest in the contents of Cosin's black box reawakened. It was hoped that Monmouth, who was a Protestant, could succeed to the throne rather than the king's brother James, an unpopular Catholic. The king had, however, denied his marriage to Lucy Walter, and his brother did become James II in 1685. The box was passed to Cosin's son-in-law after the bishop's death, but its contents seem never to have been definitively recorded. The bishop's black box remains a loose end in English history.

When Charles was restored to the throne of England in 1660 Cosin, who had been a leading Anglican light during the exile, was a natural choice for bishop of Durham, not least because he already knew the place well. As the new bishop crossed the Tees, the lord of Sockburn presented him with an ancient and particularly deadly-looking sword, of the type known as a falchion. This was supposed to be the sword used by Sir John Conyers to kill a local dragon, around the time of the Norman Conquest. The falchion can still be seen in the Durham Cathedral treasury, but it is not thought to date from as early as the eleventh century.

Cosin seems to have been impressed by the enthusiasm of the greeting he received from the people gathered to see the falchion ceremony, but he found little else to impress him in his bishopric, which had suffered badly during the civil war. During the Interregnum, when England had no resident monarch, Durham cathedral had been closed for business. After the battle of Dunbar in 1650, it had been used as a prison for some three thousand Scottish prisoners. About half of these men, who are now known as the Dunbar Martyrs, died during their imprisonment, and it is thought that as many as two thousand may have died on the march from Dunbar to Durham.

It seems that the Scottish prisoners had not been given fuel for heating, and they resorted to cutting up all the woodwork inside the cathedral and burning it to keep warm. This included much of the organ, and the woodwork in the choir.

As the first bishop after the Restoration, Cosin was responsible for some grand building projects, including the replacement of the choir woodwork in the cathedral and the installation of a remarkable wooden font-cover that still survives today. To finance these works, he set about extracting as much income as possible from his battered bishopric, and even overstepped the limits placed on the powers of the bishops of Durham under Henry VIII. In those days, Durham was not represented in Parliament, as it was considered to be a separate territory. Cosin resisted all attempts to remedy this situation, and there were no Durham MPs at Westminster during his episcopate.

Cosin was a noted scholar, and had a major part to play in such important literary endeavours as the revision of the Anglican Book of Common Prayer. He was an inveterate book-collector, and had resisted the temptation to sell off his remarkable library even during the lean times in Paris. He built Cosin's Library on the west side of Palace Green in Durham, and his coat of arms is still to be seen above the old main entrance. The arms feature a bishop's mitre, sitting inside a crown at its base. This is an ancient visual representation of the dual nature of the bishop of Durham's powers – as both a secular and a religious leader.

Despite his age (he was sixty-six when he became bishop), his ill health and his involvement with building schemes in Durham City and elsewhere, Cosin still found time to use his legal powers to persecute non-Anglicans. In the case of a local Quaker called John Longstaff, Cosin combined his interests as a persecutor and a builder. Longstaff helped Cosin build his library and the almshouse that faces it across Palace Green, but he was also imprisoned by Cosin and had money and goods confiscated as a punishment for such Quakerly crimes as non-payment of tithes.

Cosin had suffered for years from 'stone', meaning bladder stones, and he died in London in January 1672, having had several painful fits of 'stangury' or severe pain passing water. Unlike Cuthbert Tunstall, who had also died in London, Cosin was not buried there, but in the chapel of his palace at Bishop Auckland, which he had made by remodelling the old great hall.

Burned in Effigy: William Van Mildert (1826-1836)

It was during John Cosin's time as bishop of Durham that the great-grandfather of the very last of the prince-bishops was settling in England. The reader will not be surprised to learn that William Van Mildert's family were Dutch: at first they attended services of the Dutch Reformed Church, but during the eighteenth century the family became Anglicised, and Anglican.

When William announced his intention to take holy orders, the Van Milderts were not optimistic about his prospects in the Church of England. In those days Anglican clergy tended to get ahead only if they had valuable contacts among their family and friends who could get them into lucrative benefices, livings and lectureships. Since many priests benefited from several incomes held 'in plurality', their less fortunate colleagues could spend long years as poor curates. The 'pluralists' often neglected some (or even all) of the jobs for which they drew incomes, and the number of absentee priests was a national scandal. All this meant that parishes were neglected, and clergy houses, standing unoccupied for years on end, would fall into rack and ruin.

One of the most notorious absentee priests was a canon of Durham cathedral during the time that Van Mildert was bishop there. The alarmingly eccentric Francis Egerton didn't even live in England – he dwelt in Paris in a house full of cats and dogs. When he went out in his carriage, some of these animals came with him, dressed up as little ladies and gentlemen.

There was a demand for more churches and more priests, but the Church was wary about carving out new parishes which might compromise the incomes of existing clergy. As the populations of certain areas rose, the Anglican churches filled up and people were tempted to attend Baptist or other Dissenting churches and chapels. Wealthy people rented pews in Anglican churches for their exclusive use, so that sometimes a half-empty church would have to turn away worshippers.

Van Mildert's family connections proved to be more useful than anyone had expected, and he was able to build up an invaluable network of contacts by forging life-long friendships when he was a student at Oxford, and later in his working life. He was a leading member of the so-called Hackney Phalanx, an informal grouping of like-minded clergymen and lay people based in London. The Phalanx was determined to defend and promote the interests of the Church of England in its most conservative and traditional form. The members were 'high', even 'high and dry' churchmen, and they were particularly keen on maintaining and strengthening the role of bishops in the C of E.

The Hackney group, which included among its members Christopher Wordsworth, brother of William the poet, were a curiously contradictory lot. They often seemed to be deliberately restricting the success of their various enterprises by always insisting that the outcomes should be acceptable to high churchmen like themselves. An example of this was their dislike of cooperation with other Christian groups, which they regarded as heretical and invalid.

Van Mildert, the future bishop of Durham, acquired a reputation as a writer of extremely scholarly sermons and lectures, delivered with great earnestness and in a surprisingly low-pitched voice for one of his slight frame. In fact he was so scholarly that his friends invented a parlour game in his honour, which he usually won. They would read out snippets from the most obscure theological books they could find, and he would usually manage to identify them. He was also a very conscientious worker, and soon

41

he was able to increase his income by accepting various appointments. These he held in plurality, of course, but his conscientiousness forced him to make a brave attempt at doing several jobs at once, and being in more than one place at a time.

One opportunity for preferment came on a day when Van Mildert was completely unready. One evening in 1813 he was alone at his house at Farningham in Kent when a messenger arrived. The messenger found one servant in the house, who was churning butter. He asked her to fetch the master, but she refused to do so unless he, the messenger, carried on doing the churning in her place. The messenger turned out to be from the Prime Minister, Lord Liverpool, who wanted Van Mildert to be the new Regius Professor of Divinity at Oxford.

Van Mildert's high church views meant that he stood up for some pretty unpopular causes. He disapproved of the removal of the various legal restrictions on members of the Roman Catholic Church, and on members of Dissenting Churches such as the Baptists and the Quakers. He also stood up for King George IV (previously the Prince Regent) in his legal battles against his estranged wife, Caroline of Brunswick.

Caroline, whose situation was similar in some ways to that of Diana, Princess of Wales in her last years, was a popular figure, and many people felt she had been wronged by her royal husband. As a result of his support for King George, 'a tumultuous crowd of country people' attacked Van Mildert's parsonage and threw stones at the windows. The fact that he had previously reinforced the wall around the property suggests that he had been expecting trouble, or that this was not the first incident of the type that he had suffered.

As bishop of Durham, Van Mildert's opposition to the second Reform Bill of 1831 meant that he was burned in effigy at the gates of his own castle. Various local people, including members of the upper classes, spoke against him and there were threats that his windows would be broken, as they had been at Ewelme in Oxfordshire. The bishop believed that supporters of the Bill were concerned to 'watch an opportunity of doing me personal violence', and that he might end up being 'waylaid or knocked on the head', particularly if he passed through Darlington where people planned to see him 'personally maltreated'.

Van Mildert's appointment as bishop of Durham was held up as proof that people could rise to the top in the England of his time without the advantages of wealth or high birth, but the very conservative opinions of this son of a Southwark gin-distiller made him a champion of the status quo. His stand against reform made him a controversial figure, and seems to have lost him the chance of becoming archbishop of Canterbury. When moves were afoot to straighten out the finances of the Church of England by redistributing the unearned wealth of many churchmen, Van Mildert devised all sorts of ingenious arguments to persuade the government to leave things pretty much as they were.

In a letter to the bishop, the Conservative Prime Minister Robert Peel gave an example of why change was needed. He pointed out that the dean of Durham earned £9,000 a year just for being a dean, while at the same time in many parts of the county 'there is no adequate provision for the performance of the Rites of the Church'. £9,000 in 1835, when Peel wrote his letter, would be worth nearly half a million today.

The clerics of Durham were very rich at this time because the value of their lands had increased due to the mining of coal and lead in the area. The bishop was able to live in great style, with several residences and two packs of fox-hounds. Van Mildert did, however, use his money to better the cause of the Church in his diocese, for instance by building no less than fourteen new churches, and improving thirteen more. He also built and restored clergy houses, and split up some parishes into smaller parishes that were easier to manage.

Although he fought hard to defend it, Van Mildert knew that the income of the Church in Durham was excessive, and likely to be severely reduced as the spirit of reform swept through the nation. Together with Archdeacon Thorp, of whom it was said that 'his speech is like the purring of a cat, and his eye restless in its feline treachery,' Van Mildert cooked up a scheme to found a university at Durham. This was an idea that had been mooted during the Interregnum, but had not survived that turbulent time.

The new University of Durham, modelled in many ways on the more ancient universities of Oxford and Cambridge, was a child of the cathedral. It was intended, in part, as an argument in favour of the usefulness of the richly-endowed cathedral at Durham. At first its students were remarkably homogeneous, since they were all Anglicans of the male gender, and a great many of them were destined for the Church.

It is clear that, in his last days, William Van Mildert knew perfectly well that such phenomena as the prince-bishops of Durham and the embarrassing wealth of their bishopric would not survive for long after his death. Although the palace at Bishop Auckland was not 'levelled with the dust' as Van Mildert suspected it might be, William was the last of the prince-bishops. As such he ended a tradition that stretched back nearly eight hundred years, and even longer if we count the pre-Conquest bishops as prince-bishops.

From the Conquest to Van Mildert, there were fifty prince-bishops of Durham: needless to say, it would take a much longer book than this one to do them all justice. Of these, the most famous was probably Henry VIII's right-hand man Thomas Wolsey, but Wolsey, who was also a cardinal and a papal legate, never set foot in his diocese while he was bishop of Durham.

There were many periods when the see lay vacant, most notably during the Interregnum when, for a time, bishops were abolished altogether in England.

It is true that the bishops of Durham, with their combination of legal, ecclesiastical and, in less peaceful days, military powers, ruled like kings between Tees and Tyne. But few monarchs rule without some checks on their power, and the prince-bishops of Durham had to contend with rival kings in England and Scotland, and with the demands of the local aristocracy. When England was still a Roman Catholic country, the bishops sometimes had to bow to the will of the pope and his representatives. They also had to contend with their deans, archdeacons and other church officials and, until the Reformation, with the Durham monks and their prior.

44

We have seen that, in the nineteenth century, Van Mildert had to take account of the views of Parliament and the Prime Minister: he also had to keep track of public opinion as reflected in local and national newspapers, and in the activities of the mob.

The names of a few of the prince-bishops survive today because some of the colleges of Durham University, such as Hatfield and Van Mildert, have been named after them. There is also a prince-bishops primary school, a brass band, a river cruiser and a car park named for the prince-bishops. County Durham is promoted to tourists as the Land of the Prince Bishops, although many prince-bishops and prince-archbishops existed on the Continent in medieval times. It can be argued that the pope, who is bishop of Rome and also the head of state of Vatican City, is a surviving example of a prince-bishop.

List of Prince-Bishops from the Conquest to 1836

William Walcher 1071–1080
William de St Carileph 1081–1096
Ranulf Flambard 1099–1128
Geoffrey Rufus 1133–1140
William of St Barbara 1143–1153
Hugh du Puiset 1153–1195
Philip of Poitou 1197–1208
Richard Marsh 1217–1226
Richard Poore 1229–1237
Nicholas Farnham 1241–1249
Walter of Kirkham 1249-1260
Robert Stichill 1261–1274
Robert of Holy Island 1274–1283
Anthony Bek 1283–1311
Richard Kellawe 1311–1316
Lewis de Beaumont 1318–1333
Richard de Bury 1333–1345
Thomas Hatfield 1345–1381
John Fordham 1382–1388
Walter Skirlaw 1388–1405
Thomas Langley 1406–1437
Robert Neville 1438–1457
Lawrence Booth 1457–1476
William Dudley 1476–1483
John Sherwood 1484–1494

Richard Foxe 1494–1501
William Senhouse 1502–1505
Christopher Bainbridge 1507–1508
Thomas Ruthall 1509–1523
Thomas Wolsey 1523–1528
Cuthbert Tunstall 1530–1559
James Pilkington 1561–1576
Richard Barnes 1577–1587
Matthew Hutton 1589–1595
Tobias Matthew 1595–1606
William James 1606–1617
Richard Neile 1617–1628
George Monteigne 1628
John Howson 1628–1632
Thomas Morton 1632–1659
John Cosin 1660–1672
Nathaniel, Lord Crewe 1674–1721
William Talbot 1721–1730
Edward Chandler 1730–1750
Joseph Butler 1750–1752
Richard Trevor 1752–1771
John Egerton 1771–1787
Thomas Thurlow 1787–1791
Shute Barrington 1791–1826
William Van Mildert 1826–1836

Based on the list in Durham Cathedral – other lists differ, for instance different dates may be given, and some extra bishops may be included, such as William Cumin (1141-1143) who was 'intruded' into the see and never consecrated. Sometimes, different spellings or versions of bishops' names are given.

SELECT BIBLIOGRAPHY

Austin, David (ed.): *Boldon Book: Northumberland and Durham*, Phillimore, 1982

Blair, C.H.H.: *Medieval seals of the bishops of Durham*, Society of Antiquaries of Durham, 1922

Fraser, C.M.: *A history of Antony Bek*, Oxford, 1957

French, M.R.: *The prince bishops of Durham*, Durham Joint Curriculum Study Group

Hegge, Robert: *The legend of St Cuthbert*, Simon Webb, 2009

Henry of Huntingdon: *The history of the English people 1000-1154* (trans. Diana Greenway), Oxford, 2002

Jackson, Michael J. (ed.): *Engineering a cathedral*, Thomas Telford, 1993

Johnson, Margot: *John Cosin*, Turnstone, 1997

Kapelle, William E.: *The Norman Conquest of the North*, Croom Helm, 1979

Lapsley, Gaillard Thomas: *The County Palatine of Durham*, Longmans, 1900

Low, J.L.: *Historical scenes in Durham Cathedral*, Andrews, 1887

Osmond, Percy H.: *A life of John Cosin*, Mowbray, 1913

Proud, Keith: *The prince bishops of Durham*, Keybar, 1990

Rites of Durham, The (ed. James Raine), Surtees Society, 1842

Rollason, David et al (eds.): *Anglo-Norman Durham: 1093-1193*, Boydell, 1994

Rutherford, Moira: *Quakers in the City of Durham 1654-1858*, White & Co, 1997

Scammell, G.V.: *Hugh du Puiset: bishop of Durham*, Cambridge, 1956

Simeon of Durham: *A history of the church of Durham* (trans. Joseph Stevenson), Llanerch, 1993

Simeon of Durham: *A history of the kings of England* (trans. J. Stephenson), Llanerch, 1987

Stranks, C.J.: *This sumptuous church*, SPCK, 1973

Sturge, Charles: *Cuthbert Tunstal*, Longmans, 1938

Tout, T.F.: *Edward the first*, Macmillan, 1920

Webb, Simon: *Victorian Durham*, Langley Press, 2010

William of Malmesbury: *Chronicle of the kings of England* (trans. J.A. Giles), Bohn, 1847

ALSO FROM THE LANGLEY PRESS:

ISBN: 978-0954475956

ISBN: 978-0954475963

langleypress@googlemail.com